First IMPRESSIONS
Lasting IMPRESSIONS

Openings and Closings You Can Count On!

DAVE ARCH
Introduction by Bob Pike

Jossey-Bass
Pfeiffer
San Francisco

Creative Training Techniques
Press

Copyright © 1993 by Jossey-Bass/Pfeiffer and Creative Training Techniques Press

ISBN: 0-7879-5122-6

The materials that appear in this book *(except those for which reprint permission must be obtained from the primary sources)* may be freely reproduced for educational/training activities. There is no requirement to obtain special permission for such uses. We do, however, ask that the following statement appear on all reproductions:

> *First Impressions/Lasting Impressions,* by Dave Arch
>
> Copyright ©1993 by Jossey-Bass/Pfeiffer and Creative Training Techniques Press. Published by Jossey-Bass/Pfeiffer, San Francisco, CA.

This permission statement is limited to the reproduction of material for educational/training events. *Systematic or large-scale reproduction or distribution (more than one hundred copies per year)—or inclusion of items in publications for sale—may be done only with prior written permission. Also, reproduction on computer disk or by any other electronic means requires prior written permission.*

Printed in the United States of America

Published by

350 Sansome Street, 5th Floor
San Francisco, California 94104-1342
(415) 433-1740; Fax (415) 433-0499
(800) 274-4434; Fax (800) 569-0443

www.pfeiffer.com

Printing 10 9 8 7 6 5 4 3 2 1

 This book is printed on acid-free, recycled stock that meets or exceeds the minimum GPO and EPA requirements for recycled paper.

THANK YOU

To my wife, Sue, who is a partner to me
beyond my expectations.

To my close friend, Doug McCallum, who has always
believed in the power of magic.

And finally...

To the magicians whose love for magic
has refined many of the tricks
used in this book.

We apologize in advance to those magicians for
any omissions of credit. Those brought to
our attention will be corrected
in future editions.

FIRST IMPRESSIONS! and LASTING IMPRESSIONS!
–Two Books in One!–

After making your own training deck of Magic Memory Review Cards, you'll soon be bringing that deck to life in a series of proven Openings and Closings. Cards from that special deck will magically appear, disappear, and even jump out of the pack.

The deck itself will freeze into an unbelievable solid block and even disappear while held at your fingertips!

All of this happens without any difficult skills and in direct and logical support of your training content!

You'll be amazed at how easy it is to amaze!

FIRST IMPRESSIONS! Openings You Can Count On

TABLE OF CONTENTS

INTRODUCTION by Bob Pike..................v

INTRODUCTION..........................1

Learn three reasons anyone ever pays attention to anything and how those reasons can build greater strength into your openings!

> **ATTENTION:**
> Please read this next section, "Building a Magic Memory Deck" before continuing.

BUILDING A MAGIC MEMORY DECK.........7

Turn a deck of cards into a powerful review tool!

MARKED CARDS...........................9

One fun way to introduce the deck is to speak of the deck as being a deck of marked cards. The trainer shows the back of the cards and they look ordinary. However, the trainer explains that the markings can only be seen with a very special type of glasses.

The trainer puts on a goofy looking pair of glasses and reads from the back of an apparently normal card.

A member of the training group puts on the glasses and suddenly not only can she see the review questions written on the backs of the cards but so can the rest of the class! Laughter always greets the questions' sudden appearance!

First Impressions! Lasting Impressions!

FIRST IMPRESSIONS! Openings You Can Count On

Table of Contents

SOLID FUN! 11

The trainer takes the deck and gives it a shuffle. He encircles the deck with a rubber band and tosses the deck to a member of the training class

The person is told to look at any card in the deck.

Imagine his surprise when he finds that the deck has sealed itself into a solid block of cards. They are now all glued together. He can't pull out a single card! The only card he can possibly read is the back of the top card! Oh well, fortunately, the writing on this card introduces the content of the session perfectly!

NAME THAT CARD! 15

The trainer might also introduce the deck of cards by telling the class that she has been learning a card trick or two. The trainer spreads the cards so that the faces of the cards can be seen. Any person merely thinks of a card. The trainer now claims to be able to name the thought of card! As the audience member concentrates, the trainer announces that the name of the card is "role play" (or whatever content oriented word you might want to use).

Showing that the cards are indeed marked on the backs with different training techniques, the trainer asks the person to name his card. When he does call out the number and suit of his card, that card is found and on its back is indeed the term "role play!"

This is a great way to introduce the deck and give it importance to the training time! The writing on the back of the selected card can be anything desired by the trainer to help introduce training content!

FIRST IMPRESSIONS! Openings You Can Count On

Table of Contents

READY...AIM...FIRE!...........................19

This is a great way for using the deck to introduce the focus of the training session!

The deck of cards is encircled with a rubber band. Holding his hand like a gun, a volunteer takes careful aim at the deck hoping to shoot a card right out of the deck.

As he fires at the deck, the group yells "**BANG!**" and one card flies from the deck. It is a card with a burnt bullet hole right through it!

The question on the back of the card exactly corresponds to the focus of the session's content.

"In this session, we will be aiming at..." provides a perfect lead-in.

THE LAZY MAGICIAN....................23

The trainer laments the fact that he could never be a great magician because he's just too lazy to put in the practice time necessary. If he were a magician, he would do his magic like this...

The trainer trades places with a member of the audience. As the trainer sits casually in the audience, the volunteer follows the trainer's instructions. Going to the front of the room, the volunteer takes the deck of cards and following the instructions of the trainer makes a selection of a card.

The trainer now directs attention to an envelope that has been hanging from the ceiling since the trainees entered the room.

When the envelope is opened, inside is found a prediction exactly matching the card he selected! The question on the card is the focus of the content for the session! The session begins with much fun and interest!

FIRST IMPRESSIONS! Openings You Can Count On

Table of Contents

ANYONE CAN DO IT!/Part I 25

To prove that anyone can do mysterious card magic, a card is freely selected by a member of the training group and shown to all but one member of the training class. The card is replaced in the deck and handed to the one person in the group who never saw the card.

With no previous coaching, the volunteer looks through the cards and successfully locates the selected card!

But wait...this demonstration is not done yet!

ANYONE CAN DO IT!/Part II 27

The deck is now handed to still another member of the class with instructions to go to a far corner of the room and select any card in the deck. He is to then hide the card on his person and bring the deck back.

Again...the initial volunteer tells this second person the card he selected!

Now...the audience brainstorms how the magic might have been accomplished. The final understanding of this miracle serves as an excellent example for setting in place a very creative atmosphere in the training room!

FIRST IMPRESSIONS!   Introduction by Bob Pike

Introduction to First Impressions

One of the challenges that most trainers face is opening the training program or presentation with impact, that is creating the right first impression. We know that people remember what we do first best. We never get a second chance to make a favorable first impression. In Creative Training Techniques™, we suggest there are three primary tests of an effective opener. Meeting these tests will help us to have a positive first impression. First, does it break preoccupation? Does it get people mentally in the room as well as physically? Second, does it facilitate networking? Does it help people to feel less tension in the session because they're comfortable with each other? And then third, is it relevant to the program. Does it make a point?

In this collection of openers, called "First Impressions," you'll find unique ways to open a program or presentation effectively. And to create that highly favorable first impression. And you'll also find openings that allow you to score some significant points in other areas as well.

For example, openings are far more effective when they use curiosity. You'll find that here. Openings are far more effective when they're fun for both the participant and the trainer. And you'll certainly find that element incorporated into these first impressions. One thing to remember though, the most important part of any opening is the application or learning point that it makes. And that is something you're going to have to be responsible for. Remember the six p's of a powerful presentation. And that is this, proper presentation and practice prevent poor performance. So let me suggest these steps to mastering the application of any of these "First Impressions."

FIRST IMPRESSIONS! Introduction by Bob Pike

Start with one that intrigues you. One that you find interesting, unusual, etc., and begin to master the elements of performing the trick long before you ever start thinking about using it in the classroom. By the time you use it in an actual presentation, performing the trick should be second nature to you. As you practice, start thinking about: What's the point, what's the application, what's the story that I can tell that will really drive home my point. The story is the key. If you'll give yourself time to play with the trick, and get comfortable with it, you'll find the story gradually evolving as well. Your own confidence in using the trick, because it's so well practiced, is a key to making a very positive first impression.

FIRST IMPRESSIONS! Openings You Can Count On

INTRODUCTION

Why does anyone ever pay attention to anything?

What a great question for a trainer to contemplate! What causes you to give someone or something your attention? In the final analysis we are at the mercy of our trainees. They must *GIVE* us their attentions or we won't have them!

In thinking about this foundational training issue, I've become convinced that there are at least *THREE REASONS* anyone chooses to give another their attention.

Attention Reason #1: COMPELLING SENSORY INPUT

This one is as close to an involuntary response as any of the three reasons. Someone yelling "Hey you!," a loud noise, a sudden silence, a rancid smell, or an unexpected pain all demand my attention! I turn my head, I sit up, and if only for a moment, I study the situation to see what's happening. If I find that nothing significant is occurring, my mind goes back to what it was doing before the disturbance.

Consequently, this is the weakest of the three reasons.

Compelling sensory input cannot retain my attention without being combined with one of the other stronger reasons.

A trainer can certainly use a brightly colored graphic for sudden visual input or appropriate music for auditory input.

Often a skilled trainer will capture or recapture attention with the sound of their own voice. A variation in the volume of their voice (either louder or softer) or even the sudden cessation of their voice will often cause a temporary grabbing of the group's attention. Such a tactic will then need to be augmented with one of the following approaches if the arrested attentions are to be successfully held.

FIRST IMPRESSIONS! Openings You Can Count On

Introduction

Attention Reason #2: CURIOSITY

**Why did they do that?
How does it work?
What are they like?**

These questions all cause me to study a situation for a longer period of time. These are the questions that have all the potential of making me care about what's happening.

When I begin to care about something or someone, I give it value and consequently pay attention to it.

Sprinkling curiosity stimulators throughout our training is essential in keeping the attention of our trainees! When they cease being curious, they cease to care. When they cease to care, they cease to give us their full attention.

Too often trainers satisfy the curiosity of their trainees too soon (before the trainees have been made to care about the content). You can prove this to yourself by taking several small cardboard boxes and placing one common article in each box (i.e. a piece of rope, an eraser, a plastic cup, etc.). Seal each box completely so that no one can tell what's in each box and number the boxes for easier identification. Place a box on each training table.

Now give each table three minutes to shake and roll their box—seeking to make observations about what might be inside. At the end of the three minutes, have them silently record their guess as to what might be in their numbered box. Then have them try for three more minutes with another table's box.

Do this until each table has had a try at each box.

Now ask each table for their guess at each box's content. After gathering their guesses, just put the boxes away. Never confirm or deny the validity of their guesses and go on with your training. You will find that some of your trainees will become obsessed with the content of those silly little boxes. They will want to know exactly what's in each one. They will want to know if they were wrong or right. However, if you were to tell them the truth about the content of each

FIRST IMPRESSIONS! Openings You Can Count On

Introduction

box, all interest in those boxes would suddenly cease. As long as you withhold the information, you have their attention!

This is where the *SIXTY SECOND SECRET* comes into play. On the average, how long does it take you to get your training group "with you?" If you want to accomplish the job in sixty seconds or less, use curiosity to build tension *BEFORE THE SESSION BEGINS*! Begin building that curiosity as soon as your trainees enter the room!

Have something pertinent (but unusual) hanging from the ceiling, have a creative Early Bird activity on the overhead (see *Tricks For Trainers* books for many ideas!), or walk around the room placing something odd on each table (i.e. rubber bands, balloons, etc.) for use later. Give no explanation. Then don't use these items immediately. Plan to use them later in the session.

However, as you plan your curiosity stimulators, always keep one additional piece of information in mind. People are infinitely more curious about other people than they are about things. The question "What are they doing?" is more compelling to all of us than is the question "What is it?" Human beings are universally more curious about other human beings than they are about things.

Therefore, another skill to cultivate in developing curiosity in your training is that of making your training group constantly wonder about you as a person. Don't use illustrations that simply refer to "One day a dog was walking down the street..." Instead use illustrations that you have tied into personal information about yourself! The most effective openings always reveal something about you as a person in the context of your content!

Learn to make your group ask about what *YOU* are going to do next! Why did *YOU* just do what *YOU* did? Make them care about *YOU* and you will soon have them caring about what you're saying. This book will give you many ideas for use in accomplishing that task!

FIRST IMPRESSIONS! Openings You Can Count On

Introduction

Attention Reason #3: CONFLICT/RESOLUTION

If you've ever been caught up in a television program you didn't even plan to watch or been unable to put a book down until you'd finished it, you know what this reason is all about.

As an extension of curiosity, this reason holds me the longest. I want to know how the book ends, so I put off going to bed (sometimes for hours). I want to know how the movie ends, so I postpone other activities to satisfy my curiosity.

We must learn how to build conflict/resolution into our training sessions too! Like great music by Beethoven or Mozart our training must create and release tension throughout the composition/session. We must learn how to make our trainees care about the material by stimulating their curiosity and then not satisfying that curiosity until we are ready to release their attention.

Since tension with no release is uncomfortable for even the hardiest of us, the skilled trainer will build a series of conflict/resolutions within the training session. There will be many curiosity stimulators followed by curiosity satisfiers sprinkled throughout the training.

Some of the conflict we experience in training is natural conflict (i.e. felt needs). If I'm experiencing stress to an uncomfortable level, I will pay attention at a stress seminar. No one has to make me pay attention. I want to bring resolution to my conflict.

However, I am not always so naturally motivated. Some conflict must be manufactured by the trainer. I will then still pay attention to bring resolution to the conflict if the trainer helps me care about the conflict in the first place.

The openings that you find in this book have been carefully designed to maximize the use of Compelling Sensory Input, Curiosity, and Conflict/Resolution to effectively capture and hold the attention of the training group.

You will also find that all of the openings are content friendly! Each one can be modified to reflect the content you're currently teaching.

FIRST IMPRESSIONS! Openings You Can Count On

Introduction

Finally, you will notice that they can be adjusted to your personality and the personality of your group.

Realizing that there are introverted trainers as well as extroverted trainers, you will find introverted openings and extroverted openings within the pages of this book.

However, most of the openings in this book can be presented in either mode.

An *INTROVERTED OPENING* tends to use questioning in its presentation (i.e. "Have you ever seen a deck of marked cards?") in order to build curiosity.

An *EXTROVERTED OPENING* comes right at you with more of a compelling sensory experience (i.e. "I just bought a deck of marked cards!"). This also builds curiosity and tension.

Rather than only doing one type of opening, the best trainers will adjust their opening style to the group for which they're presenting. I'm sure you've noticed that groups have personalities too! Some groups are more introverted and some are more extroverted.

If you train an introverted group and use an "in your face" extroverted opening, you will drive the group members further inside themselves—defeating your hope of drawing them out into interaction.

If you have an extroverted group and you approach them with a series of introverted questions, you will quite frequently not capture their attention due to the lack of appropriate energy in your opening.

And *ENERGY* is the key word to creating a successful opening!

It doesn't always need to be the high energy that is associated with a flaming extrovert, but it needs to be energy that comes from successfully building tension—using the dynamic of our natural curiosity. This can often be a quiet and intense form of energy.

FIRST IMPRESSIONS! Openings You Can Count On

Introduction

Finally, as you play with the various openings in this book, make them your own. Process the suggested presentation through your own personality and then through the personality of your training group. As spoken of earlier, make each presentation an extension of some experience in your own life.

Then these openings will serve you well!

FIRST IMPRESSIONS! Openings You Can Count On

Please read this section before continuing.

BUILDING A MAGIC MEMORY DECK

All of the openings in this book utilize The Magic Memory Deck in one form or another. This excellent training deck is constructed by taking a full deck of playing cards and printing either review questions, terms, or even desired actions (i.e. computer skills) on the backs of the cards. For ease of reading the questions, red back decks work better than blue back decks.

When you go to purchase the deck for your Magic Review Deck, go ahead and buy four or five other duplicate decks. You'll need those decks for some of the presentations contained in this book.

Some trainers use pressure sensitive mailing labels while others prefer using a permanent marker (the Sharpie series of pens work great) to print the information on the back of the cards.

By placing the more difficult information on the backs of the higher value cards (i.e. tens, jacks, queens, kings), the answers to those questions become worth more points.

By dividing the deck into suits, the information from different phases of the training can be written on the back of the different suits.

For example, all questions from the first part of the session might be on the back of the Clubs, the second part questions on the back of the Hearts, and so on through four different sections of questions (or terms or actions).

If you don't have enough questions for an entire deck, just use as many cards as you have questions!

As is obvious now, this deck's primary use is in a series of closing reviews with table-teams drawing cards from the face up deck—seeking to answer the question on the back (or even completing the action as in computer training).

If they miss the question, the number of points on the card is deducted from their score. If they get it right, points are

FIRST IMPRESSIONS! Openings You Can Count On

Building a Magic Memory Deck

added to their score. Should they choose a higher value card with a harder question or a lower value card with a greater chance of getting it right? That's the key question of strategy!

As fun as that is...it is only the beginning of what can be done with this deck!

Believing that a good Opening and Closing are paramount to an effective training session, the magic with this deck of cards focuses on these two crucial elements—introducing the material in an interactive manner and memorably summarizing the material at the conclusion of the training session.

FIRST IMPRESSIONS! Openings You Can Count On

MARKED CARDS

One fun way to introduce the deck is to speak of the deck as being a deck of marked cards. The trainer shows the back of the cards and they look ordinary. However, the trainer explains that the markings can only be seen with a very special type of glasses.

The trainer puts on a goofy pair of glasses and reads from the back of an apparently normal card.

A member of the training group puts on the glasses and suddenly not only can she see the review questions written on the backs of the cards but so can the rest of the class! Laughter always greets the questions' sudden appearance!

Have your deck of Magic Memory Cards with two blank backed cards (no review questions on the backs) on top of the face down deck. Then underneath those two cards have the first of the genuine review cards. Select a card whose review question corresponds to the material you're planning to introduce in the training session.

Introduce the deck explaining that it is a deck of marked cards. This will pique the group's curiosity. Show the back of the top card. Of course, the group won't be able to see any markings. You explain that they would require special glasses in order to see the markings.

Put on the goofiest glasses you can find and pretend to read a content review question from the top card. Take that card away and pretend to read another question from the second blank backed card in the deck.

Ask if someone in the group would like to see how the markings look. Have them put on the glasses. It's best to select someone in the front of the room so that the rest of the group will be able to watch the person's reaction as they see the markings on the deck.

Before showing them the backs of the cards, remove the top blank backed card so that now they see the back of the review card corresponding to your content.

FIRST IMPRESSIONS! Openings You Can Count On

Marked Cards

Show them the back of the card and the entire class will begin to laugh since they also see the markings! Thumb through a few more cards so that they see markings on all the other cards. Use the first card they saw to introduce your material.

"We hope to see the answer to that question very clearly after we've concluded our training session today." This would be one way to word a transition into the material.

AN ADDITIONAL IDEA...involves using the special trick deck in the next opening Solid Fun! for this opening sequence. Now you've combined two powerful openings in one!

FIRST IMPRESSIONS! Openings You Can Count On

SOLID FUN!

The trainer takes the deck and gives it a shuffle. He encircles the deck with a rubber band and tosses the deck to a member of the training class.

The person is told to look at any card in the deck.

Imagine his surprise when he finds that the deck has sealed itself into a solid block of cards. They are now all glued together. He can't pull out a single card! The only card he can possibly read is the back of the top card! Oh well, fortunately, the writing on this card introduces the content of the session perfectly!

Take a deck of cards that matches your Magic Memory Deck and glue all but two of the cards together into a solid block.

One of the best ways of accomplishing this is to use a glue stick. Be careful to align each card carefully so that you will have a perfectly squared block when you are done. When you have completed this task, print a question on the back of the uppermost card that will correspond to the content you are introducing.

Stand in front of your training group holding the deck with your thumb and fingers holding the ends of the deck (FIGURE #1). The bottom of the face down deck is closest to your palm with the two loose cards on top of the deck.

Paying no attention to the deck, absentmindedly shuffle the cards in the following manner while giving your introductory statements.

FIGURE #1

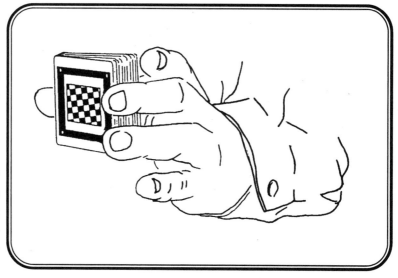

First Impressions! Lasting Impressions!

FIRST IMPRESSIONS! Openings You Can Count On

Solid Fun!

FIGURE #2

Pull off one loose card from the top of the deck with your other thumb and pull it into that hand (FIGURE #2). Pull off the other loose card in the same manner and pull it onto the first loose card. Finally, pull the entire block of cards so that they fall in front of the two loose cards.

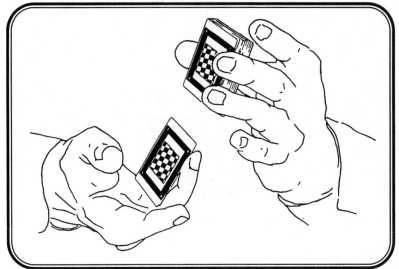

Pick up all the cards back into your original hand—holding it by the ends as in the beginning. However, now the two loose cards will be closest to your palm.

Pull off the entire block of cards with the thumb of your other hand and drop it into that other hand. Then pull off one of the single cards so that it is in front of the block of cards. Finally, pull the last single card into the front of the other cards in your other hand.

If you now pick up all the cards back into the original starting position (FIGURE #1), you will be back into the original starting position.

When you casually do the above sequence, you will be precisely simulating an overhand shuffle of the cards. It will appear to your training group that the cards are all separate and single. Don't act like there's anything wrong with the deck and they will have no reason to suspect a thing!

Tell the group that before you actually start training you want to show them a little card trick and remove the two loose cards telling the group that they will be your prediction.

Take a rubber band from your pocket and encircle the remaining block of cards—tossing them to someone in the training group. Ask them to pick any card they desire.

FIRST IMPRESSIONS! Openings You Can Count On

Solid Fun!

They will suddenly react to the fact that the cards are all stuck together!

Act surprised and ask for the deck back. Drop it on the table to show the rest of the group that indeed the cards have frozen together.

Act as though it must have been a defective deck. Suddenly notice however that the top card of the solid block contains a question that perfectly introduces your subject! Act pleased and use the question to transition into your material.

ADDITIONAL IDEAS...include using this deck in the opening entitled "Marked Cards." If you decide to go this direction you would leave one of the two loose cards blank (see the Marked Cards opening for more details).

You might also consider finishing this opening by tossing the defective deck in the suitcase and removing the deck needed for the opening "NAME THAT CARD!" You have now combined several powerful openings to introduce your material!

A special thank you to Paul Harris, creator of this routine, for his permission to include it in this book.

14 FIRST IMPRESSIONS! Openings You Can Count On

FIRST IMPRESSIONS! Openings You Can Count On

NAME THAT CARD!

The trainer might also introduce the deck of cards by telling the class that she has been learning a card trick or two. The trainer spreads the cards so that the faces of the cards can be seen. Any person merely thinks of a card. The trainer now claims to be able to name the thought of card! As the audience member concentrates, the trainer announces that the name of the card is "role play" (or whatever content oriented word you might want to use).

Showing that the cards are indeed marked on the backs with different training techniques, the trainer asks the person to name his card. When he does call out the number and suit of his card, that card is found and on its back is indeed the term "role play!"

This is a great way to introduce the deck and give it importance to the training time! The writing on the back of the selected card can be anything desired by the trainer to help introduce training content!

Take a deck that matches your Magic Memory Cards and divide the deck into two equal piles.

On the back of one set of cards print completely different content-oriented review questions or terms.

On the back of the other set of cards print the same review question or term on each card. Select a term or review question that will introduce your training session.

Re-assemble the entire deck again face down with all the different review question cards on top of the deck and all of the same review question cards on the bottom.

Tell your training group that you'd like to show them a great card trick before actually beginning the training. Select a volunteer from the group and without showing the backs of the cards, fan the lower half of the deck so that the volunteer can see the faces of the cards.

FIRST IMPRESSIONS! Openings You Can Count On

Name that Card!

It is very important that you do not fan more than the lower half of the deck! Remember the lower half of the deck has the same information on the back of each card!

Have the volunteer mentally think of one of the cards he sees without saying a word.

Close the deck and tell the volunteer that you will now attempt to tell him the name of his card!

Appear to concentrate and tell him finally that the name of his card is (use the piece of information that is on the back of all of the cards you showed him).

He will look puzzled (as he expected you to tell him a number and suit).

Realizing that he's confused, you continue to explain by showing him the backs of the top half of the deck. Explain that each card in the deck has a review question (or term, etc.) marked on it's backside. Read some of the review questions aloud.

However, be careful to not go beyond the top half of the deck when showing these cards! Remember that the bottom half has the same information on the backs.

Ask him which card he mentally selected and turn the deck face up as you seek to find it.

When you locate his card remove it from the deck, put the deck away in your pocket or briefcase, and triumphantly turn the card around to show that you indeed did name it correctly!

You can then use the card and the question on it to introduce your content to your class.

NO MATTER HOW MUCH THEY BEG...DO NOT EXPLAIN THE WORKING OF THIS TRICK TO ANYONE IN YOUR CLASS!

IT WILL BE A MUCH TALKED ABOUT TRICK THAT YOU SHOULD KEEP TO YOURSELF!

FIRST IMPRESSIONS! Openings You Can Count On

Name that Card!

By explaining its workings to your class you will only dissipate their interest, curiosity and energy! It will be counter-productive to everything you're trying to do!

MAKE SURE...that you put the deck away immediately so that later you can switch it for the real Magic Memory Deck when you get ready to do review.

AN ADDITIONAL IDEA...is to take one of the trainees into your confidence—having them play the role of the psychic and correctly naming the card! It helps build team spirit! Simply tell the person what to say when asked to name the card. Your accomplice doesn't even need to know how the trick works.

18 FIRST IMPRESSIONS! Openings You Can Count On

FIRST IMPRESSIONS! Openings You Can Count On

READY...AIM...FIRE!

This is a great way for using the deck to introduce the focus of the training session!

The deck of cards is encircled with a rubber band. Holding his hand like a gun, a volunteer takes careful aim at the deck hoping to shoot a card right out of the deck.

As he fires at the deck, the group yells "BANG!" and one card flies from the deck. It is a card with a burnt bullet hole right through it!

The question on the back of the card exactly corresponds to the focus of the session's content.

"In this session, we will be aiming at..." provides a perfect lead-in.

In preparing for this opening, select a card from your Magic Memory Cards whose question will correspond to the content you're presenting in the training session.

Prepare the card by taking a pen and pushing it through the card—making a hole in the card.

Next take a cigarette lighter and burn the hole so that it looks like a bullet might have passed through it.

Then take a rubber band (about a size 12 is perfect) and encircle the card with the rubber band at its middle (FIGURE #3).

Finally place the card in the middle of the deck and you're ready to begin.

Ask the group if anyone has ever had any experience with a hand gun. When someone does volunteer, reach into your pocket and bring out your hand forming the shape of a gun with your index finger extended and your other fingers curled into the palm.

FIGURE #3

FIRST IMPRESSIONS! Openings You Can Count On

Ready...Aim...Fire!

Explain to the group that this gun has been with you since you were a child. Walk over to the volunteer and reach out to hand it to them. Encourage them to shape their hand into a gun as they take the gun from you. Admonish them to always keep it pointed towards the ceiling. You can have a lot of fun with this!

As you move away from the person and walk back towards the front of the room, reach into your pocket as though you are getting a rubber band. As your hand comes out of the pocket, act like you have found one and come over to the deck as though you are going to encircle the deck with the rubber band.

FIGURE #4

FIGURE #5

What you are really doing is pinching the rubber band that is already around the card and pulling it up away from the deck (FIGURE #4). Then you are taking the rubber band and pulling it around one end of the deck—encircling that end of the deck (FIGURE #5).

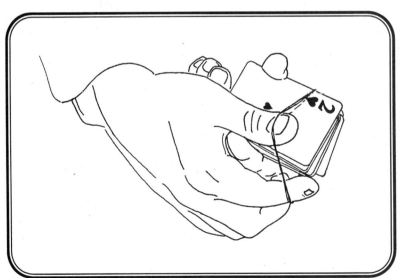

First Impressions! Lasting Impressions!

FIRST IMPRESSIONS! Openings You Can Count On

Ready...Aim...Fire!

FIGURE #6

Hold the deck as in FIGURE #6 with your index finger keeping the card from prematurely shooting out of the deck.

On the count of three have the volunteer aim at the deck and fire the gun. As a second thought remind the rest of the group that of course there will be no noise unless everyone else shouts "**BANG!**" when the gun is fired. Give them a practice shot.

Now count to three, and the volunteer will fire. Nothing happens! Look behind you as though the volunteer must have missed the deck completely.

Move closer to the volunteer and have him try again. Count to three and again it is a miss.

Come right up to the volunteer holding the deck right up against the barrel of his index finger and encourage him to try again.

This time the card goes flying into the air as you release pressure on the deck!

Drop the deck on the table (since anyone can examine it now) and go over to pick up the card. Stick your finger through the bullet hole to show that indeed damage has been done!

FIRST IMPRESSIONS! Openings You Can Count On

Ready...Aim...Fire!

Then read the question on the card. Act amazed that out of all the cards this one would have been the one shot from the deck. It perfectly introduces the topic for training!

Congratulate the marksman and begin to provide a fabulous training session in response to the question on the card!

FIRST IMPRESSIONS! Openings You Can Count On

THE LAZY MAGICIAN

The trainer laments the fact that he could never be a great magician because he's just too lazy to put in the practice time necessary. If he were a magician, he would do his magic like this...

The trainer trades places with a member of the audience. As the trainer sits casually in the audience, the volunteer follows the trainer's instructions. Going to the front of the room, the volunteer takes the deck of cards and following the instructions of the trainer makes a selection of a card.

The trainer now directs attention to an envelope that has been hanging from the ceiling since the trainees entered the room.

When the envelope is opened, inside is found a prediction exactly matching the card he selected! The question on the card is the focus of the content for the session! The session begins with much fun and interest!

Select a card from your Magic Memory Deck whose question capsulizes the content you plan to teach.

Write your prediction on a piece of paper. Indicate that you believe the volunteer will select the card with the question you've just chosen from the deck. Seal your prediction in an envelope—hanging it from the ceiling in your training room (take advantage of some natural curiosity). Don't be afraid to elaborate about how important that information is to the subject you'll be studying. Your volunteer will eventually be reading the message in its entirety to the class.

Before beginning, place the card you want the volunteer to choose on top of the face down deck.

Now think of an appropriate word to tie your training together (i.e. Quality, Training, Service, etc.). The word should be no longer than ten letters.

Hold the face down deck in your hand (with the force card on top) and spell your chosen word letter by letter dealing one card onto the table for each letter in your chosen word. Pick up your table pile and without disturbing the order, place this pile back on top of the deck.

First Impressions! Lasting Impressions!

FIRST IMPRESSIONS! Openings You Can Count On

The Lazy Magician

Your force card is now the same number down in the deck as there are letters in your chosen training word.

When you get ready to present this opening, invite a member of your training class to the front as you take their seat in the class. Tell them that you're going to have them mix the cards in a very unusual manner. Have them pick up the face down deck and lift off about one-fourth of the deck turning that group of cards face up and placing it on the top of the deck.

Now have them pick up about half of the cards in the deck turning them face up and placing them on top of the deck.

Have them spread the cards and look for the first face down card (they will find it after they pass the face up cards on top of the deck). They don't know it, but this is your original top card!

Have them remove all of the cards above this face down card. Now beginning with this first face down card (your original top card) have them deal cards one at a time face down on the table as you tell them the key training word for them to spell.

They stop on the last letter and look at that card. Have them read to the class the information on their chosen card. Then have them go to your prediction envelope and open it. Have them read your prediction message as you are given a natural lead-in to your content!

FIRST IMPRESSIONS! Openings You Can Count On

ANYONE CAN DO IT!/Part I

To prove that anyone can do mysterious card magic, a card is freely selected by a member of the training group and shown to all but one member of the training class. The card is replaced in the deck and handed to the one person in the group who never saw the card.

With no previous coaching, the volunteer looks through the cards and successfully locates the selected card!

But wait...this demonstration is not done yet!

Obtain a deck that matches your Magic Memory Deck and cover the faces of every card with a pressure sensitive mailing label so that no face on any card shows. Get large labels and trim them as needed or you might use white contact paper also.

Also make the deck appear to be just like your real Magic Memory Deck by putting review information on the backs of the cards too.

If the deck is now too thick with labels on the front and possibly on the back, take some of the cards away until the thickness of the cards is almost like that of your Magic Memory Deck.

Put this blank face deck in your coat pocket (inside coat pocket works well if you have one in your jacket).

As you begin, talk about how easy you've found magic to be. Ask for a volunteer of someone who would like to learn how to do a great card trick. When you have a volunteer, ask that person to step outside the room for just a moment while a card is selected. You don't want anyone in the rest of the training group to believe that this person could in anyway have seen or heard the name of the card about to be selected.

After this first volunteer has left the room, have another volunteer come to the front of the room and pick a card from your real Magic Memory Deck. Turn around (with the remainder of the Magic Memory Deck in your hand) as the volunteer shows the rest of the training group the card she selected.

First Impressions! Lasting Impressions!

FIRST IMPRESSIONS! Openings You Can Count On

Anyone Can Do It!/Part I

While your back is turned, drop the Magic Memory Deck in your coat pocket and withdraw the other matching blank face deck. This will not be difficult since all eyes will be on the volunteer who is showing the card, and you can go deep into a far corner of the room as a precaution against somehow glimpsing the card yourself. Then have the person who selected the card replace it in the deck (your blank faced deck) call in the volunteer from outside the room.

Have this volunteer take the deck and go into a corner—turning their back on the rest of the group as they look through the cards. Ask them to guess about which card the other person might have selected. Have them call out the number and suit of the card they believe it might have been.

The person who chose the card will be completely amazed that this amateur magician got the card right!

However, don't quit yet! The best is yet to come! See the opening "Anyone Can Do It II!"

FIRST IMPRESSIONS! Openings You Can Count On

ANYONE CAN DO IT!/Part II

The deck is now handed to still another member of the class with instructions to go to a far corner of the room and select any card in the deck. He is to then hide the card on his person and bring the deck back.

Again...the initial volunteer tells this second person the card he selected!

Now...the audience brainstorms how the magic might have been accomplished. The final understanding of this miracle serves as an excellent example for setting in place a very creative atmosphere in the training room!

The working of this part of the routine should be fairly obvious if you've taken time to read the first part of this presentation entitled "Anyone Can Do It!/Part I."

The blank faced deck is taken from the volunteer in the previous routine and handed to any other person in the training group with the instructions that they should now step out of the room and select any card they desire from the deck.

They are to bring that card into the room hidden from sight and the volunteer who correctly guessed the first card will try to tell this volunteer his card as well! Then we'll know it was more than a coincidence the first time!

When the person comes back into the room with the chosen card, the volunteer knows that there was really only one card in the deck to choose so they will have no problem guessing it correctly.

The group will be quite astonished by this person's psychic abilities!

But what if the person brings back one of the blank cards from the deck? Then the volunteer psychic will not guess correctly at first...so give him another chance. I'll bet he guesses a blank card on his second try!

Now give the group a chance to brainstorm in table groupings about how the magic might have been accomplished. In addition to generating great energy in a training room, it will really cultivate a creative atmosphere for the training to follow!

First Impressions! Lasting Impressions!

THANK YOU

To my wife, Sue, who is a partner to me
beyond my expectations.

To my close friend, Doug McCallum, who has always
believed in the power of magic.

And finally. . .

To the magicians whose love for magic
has refined many of the tricks
used in this book.

We apologize in advance to those magicians for
any omissions of credit. Those brought to
our attention will be corrected
in future editions.

First IMPRESSIONS
Lasting IMPRESSIONS

Openings and Closings You Can Count On!

DAVE ARCH
Introduction by Bob Pike

FIRST IMPRESSIONS! and LASTING IMPRESSIONS!
–Two Books in One!–

After making your own training deck of Magic Memory Review Cards, you'll soon be bringing that deck to life in a series of proven Openings and Closings. Cards from that special deck will magically appear, disappear, and even jump out of the pack.

The deck itself will freeze into an unbelievable solid block and even disappear while held at your fingertips!

All of this happens without any difficult skills and in direct and logical support of your training content!

You'll be amazed at how easy it is to amaze!

LASTING IMPRESSIONS! Closings You Can Count On

Table Of Contents

INTRODUCTION by Bob Pike..........................v

INTRODUCTION..................................1

Learn three reasons why people find activities memorable and how those reasons can build greater strength into your closings!

> **ATTENTION:**
> Please read this next section, "Building a Magic Memory Deck" before continuing.

BUILDING A MAGIC MEMORY DECK...............5

Turn a deck of cards into a powerful review tool!

WHAT'S ON YOUR MIND?........................7

A great way to get complete group involvement in the summarization of material is to finish by allowing a volunteer to select a card from the deck—attempting to get the rest of the training group to read his mind!

When the entire group in unison successfully gives him the answer to the review question on the back of his selected card, the expression on that volunteer's face is total unbelief!

The writing on the card can be anything needed to finish the session with a summarization of the content. The verbalization in unison of the entire group really makes the summarization memorable for all!

CARD ON THE BACK............................11

The title of this magic trick tells all! In the process of teaching a member of the class a card trick, the chosen card disappears from the deck and re-appears stuck to the back of the volunteer!

This selected card can have any writing desired on its back to

LASTING IMPRESSIONS! Closings You Can Count On

Table of Contents

help summarize content. The magic trick also serves as a great tool for illustrating how different persons' perspectives can help us all.

This point is graphically demonstrated since the audience does indeed see the card before the volunteer is aware of its presence!

Another benefit of this great piece of magic is that the selected card can actually be made to appear *ANYWHERE* desired to help give the trainer's emphasis additional visual impact!

TRIPLE COINCIDENCE..........................15

The deck of cards is fanned so that one person can see the cards. He mentally remembers any card he sees. Another person is given the opportunity to remember any card from the fan too. Finally, the trainer looks the cards over and selects one for himself.

At the count of three...all three people call out the card in their mind! They have all thought about the same card!

There are no duplicates in the deck! Each person could think of any card he saw! How is it possible? When the training group is shown how it works, there is much room for a summarizing application within the explanation.

CRAZY QUIZ 17

This very funny routine has the appearance of genuinely using the deck for a review session. However, it is soon apparent that something is wrong—one team member keeps getting all the easy questions while the others keep getting only impossibly hard questions!

The consolation prizes are hilarious for the losers and the entire time ends with everyone wide awake and ready to learn again!

This is perfect magic to keep in your briefcase to use when the group looks like they're starting to get sleepy! It's a great energizer to use just before going to break!

LASTING IMPRESSIONS! Closings You Can Count On

Table of Contents

VIDEO CARD TRICK! 31

The trainer finishes the session with a card trick performed by a great magician from the past.

The magician's voice on the tape (either audio or video) gives instructions as a volunteer follows those instructions with a deck of cards.

Unbelievable as it seems, the card selected by the volunteer is revealed to him by the voice on the tape!

In fact, the card selected by the volunteer is the very message card needed to summarize the material under discussion!

FINGERTIP VANISH!...............................35

The trainer holds the deck of review cards in his hand and asks any person to name any card in the deck, and it will be made to vanish!

The trainer squeezes the deck in his hand and indeed the *ENTIRE DECK* disappears without a trace...right at his fingertips!

This shocking trick can be used very well to conclude a training session. As the trainer vanishes the deck, he makes a tossing motion towards the trainees indicating that the information in the deck has now been transferred into the minds of the learners. The deck is no longer needed.

It's a very powerful way to get rid of the review deck at the end of the session!

BIOGRAPHY OF THE AUTHOR...........................39

LASTING IMPRESSIONS! Closings You Can Count On

Let's Start a List: Introduction to Lasting Impressions

Trainers frequently don't close presentations at all. They simply run out of time before they run out of content. Some say, "Well, that's all we have time for, thanks for coming," and leave participants with a real sense of incompleteness. Mastering some of these "Lasting Impressions" can help any trainer avoid this problem. In Creative Training Techniques™, we suggest there are at least two major considerations for an effective close. One, it needs to allow for celebration. We want the program to end on an up note with participants feeling good about themselves. Secondly, it should tie things together. I think that you will find that this collection of "Lasting Impressions" can help you do exactly that. They each provide you with one last opportunity to drive home and reinforce a major learning point.

One important key though is to remember you need sufficient time to close. On a full day program, for example, that's scheduled to end at 4:00, I'll act as if it's going to end at 3:30. That way if questions, heavy involvement by participants, etc., throws your program off schedule, you'll still have time for an effective close.

Each of these "Lasting Impressions" is simple. Give yourself the time to practice each "Lasting Impression" that you want to use. Once you feel comfortable with the mechanics of your closing activity, then focus on the application story. It is what we say as we're performing that really creates the impact and application. In the two, three, four or maybe five minutes that a "Lasting Impression" takes, we can reinforce content over and over without participants really being aware of it. So, select one "Lasting Impression," practice it, master it. As you've mastered one, use it to make that last final impact.

Remember, people remember what we do last, so take the time to prepare and master an effective lasting impression.

LASTING IMPRESSIONS! Closings You Can Count On

INTRODUCTION

"I ONCE SAW A MAGICIAN WHO ..."

As soon as people learn that I enjoy magic, they have a story to tell. The story usually begins with the above words, but then the endings vary.

I always listen carefully. I'm very curious as to what lifts one trick so far above the others that the viewer wants to describe it to other people they meet.

If only there were some common ingredients in those descriptions that we could use to create equally memorable training! What a difference that could make!

Whether the person is telling me about a magician who pulled a coin from their ear, burned their dollar bill, or sawed them in half, I have been able to locate three common factors from which we can learn!

Every description someone has brought to me always focused on magic that was...

SIMPLE

"That magician just broke my watch and fixed it again!"

"He just reached into the air and made money appear!"

"Those solid rings would just link and unlink!"

Every trick that's been related to me has always been very easy to describe.

No one yet has ever approached me to say...

"First, the magician had me count fifteen cards into one pile and then divide the rest of the deck into two piles. Then he had me move three cards from one pile onto the other pile and ..."

If our trainees don't have a hook for summarizing our content in the simplicity of a slogan, they will have great difficulty in remembering the main emphasis of what we were trying to say.

LASTING IMPRESSIONS! Closings You Can Count On

Introduction

Lack of a simple POINT is one of the three greatest Closing Killers!

The very nature of the closings in this book will force you to condense your training experience into one or two words! It's a great discipline for even the most technical training! It gives trainees a mental hook on which they can hang the multitude of details you've covered in the session. It gives them a string to tie around the training so that they can take it with them.

Although you'll receive an excellent tool for review as you make and use your Magic Memory Cards, the closings in this book were not designed to be review of material. That's another subject all together. These closings serve as a final pointed emphasis of one central theme that brings unity to your training session.

SPECTATOR CENTERED

The stories that others tell me about magicians usually have something personal happening to the storyteller (or at least to someone they know well)! The person telling the story has either been emotionally and/or physically involved with the magic!

As we translate that finding to our training, we find that lack of PUNCH is the second most common Closing Killer!

The closings in this book utilize the most powerful punch— personal involvement. Many of them involve the group in a visual manner. Some involve everyone physically. Hopefully, all involve the trainees emotionally through the vehicle of curiosity, conflict, and resolution (see the introduction to First Impressions! for a greater expansion on these themes).

Maximum punch in your closings results from directly involving your trainees physically and emotionally.

SPONTANEOUS

Finally, it has been interesting to me just how many of the tricks I hear people describe tend to be outside of the planned show of a typical magician.

LASTING IMPRESSIONS! Closings You Can Count On

Introduction

"He just picked up that broken rubber band and put it back together!" or "When he accidentally dropped my watch and stepped on it, I thought it was ruined, but he fixed it!"

There is an air of spontaneity to the most memorable proceedings! The magic appeared to "just happen" within the natural flow of events.

Now I don't believe for a moment that the magic did just happen. However, the wise magician was willing to hide his preparation (which maybe was quite extensive) so that the illusion of spontaneity could be created and the magic become more memorable.

In trainers talk, we translate this to mean that lack of *PLAN* is the third and final Closing Killer! Too many trainers don't take time to plan their closings!

REMEMBER: *GOOD CLOSINGS DON'T JUST HAPPEN...BUT THE BEST CLOSINGS SEEM LIKE THEY DO!*

Anytime the trainer can extensively plan and then make it appear as though s/he is stepping outside the canned presentation for a moment of spontaneity, the group sits up and takes notice. It may be a thought that apparently just struck the trainer. It may be something that appears to be going wrong for the trainer. Or it may even truly be an unplanned (and sometimes unwelcomed) comment or action from someone in the training group.

Any of these spontaneous occurrences has the potential of lifting any closing out of the ordinary and into the memorable!

A wise trainer will not only take full advantage of the opportunity but will also plan spontaneously appearing incidents within the training session!

The closings in this book are examples of how to combine those most powerful ingredients of *SIMPLICITY, SPECTATOR INVOLVEMENT,* and *SPONTANEITY* to create memorable moments for your trainees.

Then surely someday someone will say about you...

"I ONCE SAW A TRAINER WHO ..."

4 LASTING IMPRESSIONS! Closings You Can Count On

LASTING IMPRESSIONS! Closings You Can Count On

> **Please read this section before continuing.**

BUILDING A MAGIC MEMORY DECK

All of the closings in this book utilize The Magic Memory Deck in one form or another. This excellent training deck is constructed by taking a full deck of playing cards and printing either review questions, terms, or even desired actions (i.e. computer skills) on the backs of the cards. For ease of reading the questions, red back decks work better than blue back decks.

When you go to purchase the deck for your Magic Review Deck, go ahead and buy four or five other duplicate decks. You'll need those decks for some of the presentations contained in this book.

Some trainers use pressure sensitive mailing labels while others prefer using a permanent (the Sharpie series of pens work great) marker to print the information on the back of the cards.

By placing the more difficult information on the backs of the higher value cards (i.e. tens, jacks, queens, kings), the answers to those questions become worth more points.

By dividing the deck into suits, the information from different phases of the training can be written on the back of the different suits.

For example, all questions from the first part of the session might be on the back of the Clubs, the second part questions on the back of the Hearts, and so on through four different sections of questions (or terms or actions).

If you don't have enough questions for an entire deck, just use as many cards as you have questions!

As is obvious now, this deck's primary use is in a series of closing reviews with table-teams drawing cards from the face up deck—seeking to answer the question on the back (or even completing the action as in computer training).

If they miss the question, the number of points on the card is deducted from their score. If they get it right, points are

LASTING IMPRESSIONS! Closings You Can Count On

Building a Magic Memory Deck

added to their score. Should they choose a higher value card with a harder question or a lower value card with a greater chance of getting it right? That's the key question of strategy!

As fun as that is...it is only the beginning of what can be done with this deck!

Believing that a good Opening and Closing are paramount to an effective training session, the magic with this deck of cards focuses on these two crucial elements—introducing the material in an interactive manner and memorably summarizing the material at the conclusion of the training session.

LASTING IMPRESSIONS! Closings You Can Count On

WHAT'S ON YOUR MIND?

A great way to get complete group involvement in the summarization of material is to finish by allowing a volunteer to select a card from the deck—attempting to get the rest of the training group to read his mind!

When the entire group in unison successfully gives him the answer to the review question on the back of his selected card, the expression on that volunteer's face is total unbelief!

The writing on the card can be anything needed to finish the session with a summarization of the content. The verbalization in unison of the entire group really makes the summarization memorable for all!

Take your deck of Magic Memory Cards and insert an extra card from a matching deck. On this card put a three, four, or five letter word that would serve as a good summary word for closing your training session (i.e. Strive, Dare, Enjoy, Relax, Do It!, etc.).

Now cut this card about ⅛" shorter than the other cards in the deck. Also round the corners again to help disguise its shortness. Hold the deck face down and insert this special card face down about ¼ of the way down in the deck.

Then obtain what is commonly referred to as a stenographer's pad and on the back cover print in very large block letters the word that is on the card you just inserted in the deck.

Fold the cover back on the pad to hide the writing and have a marking pen or crayon within easy reach.

When ready to begin this demonstration, invite a volunteer to join you in the front of the training group and indicate that you will now attempt to have the entire group read their mind! They'll want to be careful with what they think about in the next few moments!

Take your Magic Memory Deck face down in your hand. Use the other hand to riffle the end of the cards *FROM THE BOTTOM TO THE TOP*. Because one of the cards is short, you will feel a slight bump and hear a slightly louder click as

LASTING IMPRESSIONS! Closings You Can Count On

What's On Your Mind?

that card goes by in your riffle. When you feel that, you know the deck is ready for what is to follow.

If you can't feel that click of the short card, then either your short card needs to be cut shorter or you need to tap the opposite end of the deck on a table so that the short card is tapped away from the end you're riffling.

Riffle the deck in the manner above as you ask the volunteer to simply say "Stop" anytime she desires. Go fast the first time and then notice that she didn't say "Stop" fast enough. She should really be ready to jump in quickly the second time.

When she says "Stop" confidently let the rest of the cards fall until you feel the hard click of the short card. Stop at the click and lift off the top part of the deck, turn your head away, and extend the bottom part of the deck for her to take the card. The person will take away the forced short card. This is really quite easy when you practice a few moments with the deck.

Hand the person the pad and a marking pen asking her to write the word or words on the pad. You turn your back at this point. Ask her to tear off the paper and hide it before you turn around.

Turn around and take back the pad and pen from her. Don't look at the pad! Simply put the pen back in your pocket.

Casually close the pad as you continue to talk about how this person will now attempt to send her thoughts into the minds of the training group.

Hold the pad casually at your side with the back of the pad facing the training group.

You are standing slightly ahead of your volunteer so that there is no way she can see the word on the pad's back.

Ask the audience to concentrate. When you count to three, they are to call out the first letter they sense in their minds. They will see the word on the pad and start to get the idea!

LASTING IMPRESSIONS! Closings You Can Count On

What's On Your Mind?

Your volunteer will almost collapse when the group successfully calls out the first letter of her word!

Ask her if it is correct and then proceed in the same manner with the second, third, fourth and other letters. After about the third letter, you can throw the pad into your briefcase—getting it out of the way of any suspicion.

Even when the last letter has been discerned, act as though there might be more and try again. At the count of three, you will be met with complete silence from the group. This is really quite dramatic! The word is indeed finished! Thank the volunteer for a most successful demonstration.

Then thank the group for successfully closing the training with a good one word reminder of what the training was all about!

10 LASTING IMPRESSIONS! Closings You Can Count On

LASTING IMPRESSIONS! Closings You Can Count On

CARD ON THE BACK

The title of this magic trick tells all! In the process of teaching a member of the class a card trick, the chosen card disappears from the deck and re-appears stuck to the back of the volunteer!

This selected card can have any writing desired on its back to help summarize content. The magic trick also serves as a great tool for illustrating how different persons' perspectives can help us all.

This point is graphically demonstrated since the audience does indeed see the card before the volunteer is aware of its presence!

Another benefit of this great piece of magic is that the selected card can actually be made to appear ANYWHERE desired to help give the trainer's emphasis additional visual impact!

Before presenting this illustration, take your Magic Memory Cards and remove one card from the deck whose review question summarizes the content of your training session.

If you don't have a card that quite fits that description, make an extra card from a matching deck. However, when you do use another card, be sure and remove the duplicate of that matching card (i.e. number and suit) from your Magic Memory Card deck.

Put a fresh piece of double sided tape on back top edge of your chosen card. Encircle the rest of the deck with a rubber band and lay the taped card face down loosely on top of the rubber banded face down deck. Keep this out of sight until you're ready to begin.

Ask if anyone would like to learn a truly great card trick and invite them to join you in the front of the room.

As they come to the front of the room scoop your hand under the deck and lift up both the deck and the loose card on top so that the deck is resting face down on the palm of

LASTING IMPRESSIONS! Closings You Can Count On

Card On The Back

your hand. Keep the back of your hand towards the audience. Have your hand hanging loosely at your side.

As your volunteer approaches the front of the room, use the hand that holds the deck to position the person exactly where you want them to stand.

"Please stand right here," you say to the volunteer as your free hand is placed on the volunteer's arm and the hand with the deck is placed on their back to help position them where you want them.

Press the deck against their back, and the card will stick to their back as your hand comes away with the rest of the banded deck.

Remember at this point, the group has no idea what you're about to do. There will be no suspicion! The hard part is over while the group waits for the presentation to begin!

Take the rubber band from the deck and explain to the assistant that you will tell them exactly what to say as they learn each stage of this great trick.

You will now lean over and whisper to the volunteer exactly what they are to say. They will then repeat what you've told them to say. The repetition of this process becomes very funny as the presentation continues.

You begin by whispering, "Pick a card." She says to you, "Pick a card."

You ask "May I pick any card at all?" You whisper "yes" to her and she says "yes" back to you.

You reach into the deck and pull out a card (any card) and look at the card. However, don't show the face to anyone else in the group!

You whisper, "Remember your card." She says to you, "Remember your card."

You say, "I will."

LASTING IMPRESSIONS! Closings You Can Count On

Card On The Back

You whisper, "Put the card back in the deck and shuffle the deck." She says to you "Put the card back in the deck and shuffle the deck."

You do just as she asked you to do.

You whisper to her, "I am now going to make your card disappear." She says to you "I am now going to make your card disappear."

"You are?" you ask.

Lean over and whisper "yes" to her and then she says "yes" back to you.

Whisper "When I say 'Go!' the card will disappear!" She says, "When I say 'Go!' the card will disappear!"

Whisper "Go!" She says, "Go!"

Whisper "What was your card?" She asks you "What was your card?"

Tell her that your card was the _____
(Don't name the card you really picked! Instead name the number and suit of the card you've stuck to her back).

You can't believe that the card could really be gone so you immediately begin to look through the cards (with her looking on) and discover that the card is indeed gone!

"Where did it go?" you ask your volunteer. At this point just wait patiently for a response. She will usually say something like "I don't know" or "I'm not sure."

"No! No!" you correct her. "You're suppose to say 'It's on my back!'" Now wait for her to respond to what you've just told her to say. It will be truly funny as she processes what she's about to say.

She will probably say it in the form of a question "It's on my back?"

Turn her around and show the group the card. Remove it, show it to her, and congratulate her on a job well done!

She gets the applause as she returns to her seat!

LASTING IMPRESSIONS! Closings You Can Count On

Card On The Back

Suddenly, you're pleased to notice that the question on the back of the card exactly summarizes the training you've just completed! Imagine that! Thank her for giving you such a great way to end the session!

ADDITIONAL IDEAS...will present themselves when you realize that the card could actually be hidden anywhere and in anything! Get creative! Hide it in something that will relate well to your content (i.e. under a computer, inside someone's pocket or purse, taped under someone's chair, etc.)

LASTING IMPRESSIONS! Closings You Can Count On

TRIPLE COINCIDENCE

The deck of cards is fanned so that one person can see the cards. He mentally remembers any card he sees. Another person is given the opportunity to remember any card from the fan too. Finally, the trainer looks the cards over and selects one for himself.

At the count of three...all three people call out the card in their mind! They have all thought about the same card!

There are no duplicates in the deck! Each person could think of any card he saw! How is it possible? When the training group is shown how it works, there is much room for a summarizing application within the explanation.

This is one that you will first perform and then have the training group brainstorm the possible methodology. It always creates energy and interaction. They always enjoy being let in on the secret!

Before beginning, take your Magic Memory Cards and place on the bottom of the face down deck a card whose question will summarize your training session.

Invite two people to join you in front of the room. A man and a woman works great. Place them in two positions where there is a distance between them. In a moment you will ask each of them to select a card—not showing it to anyone else.

Go to your first volunteer and hold the deck of Magic Memory Cards up to her face so that only she can see the faces of the cards. The backs of the cards face the rest of the training group.

Fan the cards in front of her face. However, fan the cards in the opposite direction from the way you would normally fan them. Now when she looks at the faces of the cards, all of the numbers and pips are hidden with the exception of the bottom card (FIGURE #7 on page 16).

Ask her to remember any card she sees. The wording of that request is very important. Usually by giving her a knowing look she will play right along with you!

LASTING IMPRESSIONS! Closings You Can Count On

Triple Coincidence

FIGURE #7

Then move to the other assistant and use the same procedure on him asking him to remember any card he sees.

Finally, turn the deck over and look through the cards yourself and pull the bottom card from the fan as you make your selection.

On the count of three have each person call out the number and suit of their selected card as you turn your chosen card around. The group will be amazed that all three chose the same card.

How can that be?

Let the group brainstorm their way to a solution!

After a solution has been realized, look down at the card as an after thought and act surprised! The question on the card exactly summarizes the content from the session! Thank your assistants for being so cooperative!

LASTING IMPRESSIONS! Closings You Can Count On

CRAZY QUIZ

This very funny routine has the appearance of genuinely using the deck for a review session. However, it is soon apparent that something is wrong—one team member keeps getting all the easy questions while the others keep getting only impossibly hard questions!

The consolation prizes are hilarious for the losers and the entire time ends with everyone wide awake and ready to learn again!

This is perfect magic to keep in your briefcase to use when the group looks like they're starting to get sleepy! It's a great energizer to use just before going to break!

This routine is very easy to do!

The description of the routine will take some time but the mechanics are simple!

If you can riffle the end of a deck of cards, you will have a fun interlude to use with your training!

Once you learn the mechanics, you can modify the questions to actually reflect content subject matter (see ADDITIONAL IDEAS).

Equipment Needed

Supplied with this book is:
1) An Answer Sheet For The Judge
2) A Certificate For The Final Award
3) A Printed Description Of The Routine And Methodology

You will also need for consolation prizes:
1) A penny
2) A round washer (the bigger the better)
3) A paper towel
4) A safety pin
5) A dime
6) An old ring or broach box

LASTING IMPRESSIONS! Closings You Can Count On

Crazy Quiz

The only additional requirements will be a deck of cards to match you Magic Memory Card deck, a tape player (see Additional Ideas), and four chairs arranged in a row for the contestants to occupy during the contest.

Preparation

1) Take twenty cards that match your Magic Memory Cards and cut ten of them 1/8" shorter than the other ten. Round the corners of those short cards so that they again appear like the other cards.

2) Look ahead in this routine and find the judge's list of questions. On the back of the long cards, put the odd numbered harder questions. On the back of the short cards, put the even numbered easy questions. Be sure to also include the number of the question on the card.

3) Now alternate the short and long cards to make your quiz deck.

4) *YOU WILL NOW DISCOVER THE SECRET THAT MAKES THIS ROUTINE WORK.* Tap the end of the deck on a table so that all of the short cards drop to one end of the deck. Then holding the deck face down, riffle the other end of the deck from top to bottom.

   If you look into the end of the deck as the cards riffle pass, you will notice that you only can see the long cards (with the harder questions).

   If you then reverse riffle the deck (from the bottom to the top), you will find that you can now only see the short cards (with the easier questions).

   You will use this unique feature to force your contestants to either choose hard or easy questions!

5) Make a copy of the Judge's Official Answer Sheet and the Certificate Of Award (you will actually print the winner's name on the certificate before the contest begins!).

LASTING IMPRESSIONS! Closings You Can Count On

Crazy Quiz

The Routine

ROUTINE OUTLINE

I. Opening Announcement
II. Trainer Introduces The Audience Contestants
III. Trainer Explains The Rules
VI. Trainer Introduces The Judge
V. The First Question (Hard Question)
VI. The Consolation Prize
VII. The Second Question (Hard Question)
VIII. The Consolation Prize
IX. The Third Question (Easy Question)
X. The Fourth Question (Easy Question)
XI. The Fifth Question (Hard Question)
XII. The Sixth Question (Easy Question)
XIII. The Consolation Prize
XIV. The Grand Prize Certificate

THE ROUTINE ITSELF

I. Opening Announcement

It seems to work best to open this section with a few quick words from the trainer to get the audience ready for the contest.

"Now…we come to a very exciting part of the program! I'm going to step out for just a moment to get ready and then we'll begin."

You could make your entrance with the flair of a gameshow host. You might even consider a flashy jacket, hat, or sunglasses to costume appropriately.

LASTING IMPRESSIONS! Closings You Can Count On

Crazy Quiz

II. Trainer Introduces The Audience Contestants

These names will need to be gathered ahead of time. You will want people who are:

    A. Relaxed In Front Of People
    B. Good Sports (They Will Be Losing)
    C. Not Too Shy Or Too Extroverted In Their Behavior

We would also suggest selecting *THREE MEN AND ONE WOMAN*. The dynamics in that formula help make the routine click. The woman immediately becomes the underdog and the audience wants to see her win! And the judge will be a woman and there will be a by-play between the two women that makes it even more fun!

The contestants don't need to know about their involvement ahead of time.

The contestants should be invited to the front and seated in the four chairs there for them.

From left to right in the eyes of the audience, they should be seated:

MAN   MAN   MAN   WOMAN

You should stand over to the side of the row so as not to obscure the view of the audience. You will want them to see the reactions of each contestant.

III. Trainer Explains The Rules

Please keep this short and simple. A long speech here will ruin the flow of the routine and dissipate the energy. Pick up the deck and begin.

Something like this will be enough:

"Allow me to quickly cover for you the rules of our contest. Here I have in my hand an envelope filled with questions. One at a time the contestants will be allowed to draw a question from the envelope. They will be given five seconds to think about their answer. They will then give their answer. The judge's decision as to the correctness of their answer will be final. Let me introduce to you our judge."

First Impressions! Lasting Impressions!

LASTING IMPRESSIONS! Closings You Can Count On

Crazy Quiz

IV. Trainer Introduces The Judge

The judge you select is important from several standpoints. They must be credible to the audience. Any authority person in the group would be acceptable. She must be able to act as though she is taking her job very seriously. We believe that a woman is better suited to this position as she interplays with the other woman and the men better.

She needs to thoughtfully look up all the answers (both easy and hard) giving pause before signalling the correctness of an answer. She needs to take her time on both the easy and the hard questions.

She should be placed in such a position that she is visible to a majority of the group.

If this is ever presented on a stage, we would suggest placing the judge standing on the floor over to one side.

In introducing the judge, again a quick introduction is best:

"We're happy to have _____ acting as our judge. She (he) has been given a list of questions with the correct answers. She (he) will signal me at the conclusion of each answer as to the correctness of the answer. Are you contestants ready to begin?"

V. The First Question

Ask the first man in the first chair on the left to stop you as you riffle the cards.

IMPORTANT: *BE SURE AND TAP THE CARDS ON ITS END EACH TIME SO THAT THE SHORT CARDS SETTLE TO ONE END OF THE DECK.*

Riffle the cards from the top to the bottom of the face down deck and this contestant will stop you at a difficult question. Remove the card and have him read the question to himself and hand the question to you. You will turn and read it to the audience.

Turn towards him and tell him to begin thinking.

LASTING IMPRESSIONS! Closings You Can Count On

Crazy Quiz

Focus your attention on him. Laughs will begin to come from the audience as he tries to act occupied with a question for which he is hopeless to generate any answer.

Ask him for his answer, check with the judge, wait for the judge's response, and indicate how sorry you are that he didn't give the right answer.

However, you don't want him to go home empty handed. He needs to stand up and you will give him his consolation prize.

THE PATTERN YOU HAVE JUST READ ABOVE IS THE TYPICAL PATTERN FOR EACH OF THE CONTESTANTS. LEARN THIS PATTERN WELL. WE WILL SIMPLY REFER BACK TO THIS ORDER AS WE DESCRIBE THE REMAINING CONTESTANT SECTIONS.

VI. The Consolation Prize

Say something like "This contestant receives a very special prize. We want to send him home with an engraved copper bust of our sixteenth President—Abraham Lincoln."

Reach into your pocket and sheepishly remove a penny. Make sure the audience sees what it is, point to Lincoln's bust on the penny, and give it to the man to take back to his seat. Lead in the applause as he returns to his place in the training group.

VII. The Second Question

"Ah, but we do have three contestants left. We'll let you go next."

Now the next man in line is forced to draw a difficult question.

Repeat the procedure exactly as with the first man. Of course he loses.

LASTING IMPRESSIONS! Closings You Can Count On

Crazy Quiz

VIII. The Consolation Prize

This man too should stand to receive his prize.

Simply say "This contestant receives a brand new washer and drier with our thanks for being a part of our show."

Look around as though expecting to see it come out of the doorway. Reach into one pocket and remove a washer (as in plumber's washer) and reach into the other pocket and remove a paper towel.

Give them to him and lead in the applause as he returns to his seat.

IX. The Third Question

Now turn your attention back to those remaining. Only two people remain.

Now riffle the deck from the bottom to the top so that the man stops you on an *EASY QUESTION!*

Follow the procedure exactly as before except of course, the judge will signal that the answer is correct!

Start the audience clapping, congratulate the man, and begin to close the contest…suddenly realizing that you never gave the woman a chance.

Apologize and proceed to the woman—giving her a chance to tie the game.

X. The Fourth Question

As you move towards the woman, riffle the cards from bottom to top so that she stops you on an *EASY QUESTION!*

Proceed as before with the judge giving serious deliberation before giving a positive signal.

"We are now in a tie breaker situation. We will give the man one more chance."

LASTING IMPRESSIONS! Closings You Can Count On

Crazy Quiz

XI. The Fifth Question

This time riffle the cards from the top to the bottom so that the gentleman draws a *DIFFICULT QUESTION*.

Proceed as before and indicate that the answer was incorrect.

BUT WAIT...the woman will need to answer a question correctly if she is to win fair and square. The man should be encouraged to remain seated while the woman attempts to answer the question she draws.

XII. The Sixth Question (Easy Question)

This time the woman will stop you on an *EASY QUESTION*.

Encourage her to take her time as this is a most important answer. She just could be the Grand Prize Winner!

Proceed as before and indicate that the answer was correct.

After she answers correctly, excitedly lead the audience in applause.

"She is the winner of our contest!" Invite both of the contestants to stand for the awarding of the prizes.

XIII. The Consolation Prize

Turn to the gentleman and indicate that you do indeed have a consolation prize for him.

"For this lucky contestant we have one of our finest prizes. We proudly award you a stunning silver dime and pin (diamond pin)."

Reach into a pocket and remove a jeweler's case. Open it and hand the gentleman a dime with the comment "Here sir is the dime." Handing him the safety pin, you exclaim, "And this is the pin...a stunning silver dime and pin."

Lead in the applause as he leaves the stage.

LASTING IMPRESSIONS! Closings You Can Count On

Crazy Quiz

XIV. The Grand Prize

Turn to the woman and remove the Certificate of Award. Read it to her out loud, hand it to her with a grandiose gesture of honor, and lead in the tumultuous applause as she returns to her seat.

The fact that it is already filled out with her name is the final signal to the training group that this was indeed a fixed contest (if there was any doubt remaining).

ADDITIONAL IDEAS

1) Equip the judge with a bell to ring for a right answer and an airhorn to blow for a wrong answer. Demonstrate these sounds during her introduction. In this case, she does not need to give any verbal cue—the sound will be enough. Airhorns are available at boating supply stores.

2) Customize the questions for real content review! However, have impossibly difficult questions for the long cards and elementary simple questions for the short cards.

3) Use music from the Game Section of the music tapes entitled "Powerful Presentation Music Tapes" available from the publisher. These tapes require no copyright permission for their use and give you excellent musical interludes to insert at the opening or during the "thinking time" for each contestant.

THE ABRIDGED VERSION

There are times when you won't want to have the game run as long as the first routine published in this book. Not a problem.

Simply have four or even three people come up from the audience. Have everyone but the last one (the woman) choose from the difficult side of the envelope with the final person choosing from the difficult side of the envelope.

LASTING IMPRESSIONS! Closings You Can Count On

Crazy Quiz

THE CRAZY QUIZ JUDGE'S
OFFICIAL ANSWER SHEET

DEAR JUDGE: Although it will take you no time at all to look up the answers to these questions, please take your time on both the easy and the hard ones. Play your part as seriously as possible. Thank you.

1. Q. If a hen and a half lays an egg and a half in a day and a half, how many and a half, who lay better by a half, lay a half-score and a half in a week and a half?
   A. No Answer Is Correct

2. Q. What Is Your Favorite Color?
   A. Any Answer Is Correct

3. Q. With six sticks of equal length, how can you form four equal-sided triangles without breaking or cutting the sticks?
   A. No Answer Is Correct

4. Q. What Is Your Favorite Song?
   A. Any Answer Is Correct

5. Q. Bill and his brother Jim have combined ages of 30. In fourteen years Jim will be three times the age Bill is now. How old is Jim?
   A. No Answer Is Correct

6. Q. What Is Your Favorite Dessert?
   A. Any Answer Is Correct

7. Q. Friday the thirteenth is reputed to be a very unlucky day. On the average, over a period of years, how frequently does Friday the thirteenth occur?
   A. No Answer Is Correct

8. Q. What Is Your Favorite Pet?
   A. Any Answer Is Correct

LASTING IMPRESSIONS! Closings You Can Count On

Crazy Quiz

9. Q. Tomorrow today will be yesterday, and yesterday today was tomorrow. When tomorrow is yesterday, today will be as near to Sunday as today was when yesterday was tomorrow. What day is it according to these facts?
   A. No Answer Is Correct

10. Q. What Is Your Favorite Drink?
    A. Any Answer Is Correct

11. Q. If a man says that he forgets what he does not wish to remember, does he mean to say that he does not remember what it is that he wishes to forget? or that he is able to forget that which he does not wish to remember?
    A. No Answer Is Correct

12. Q. What Is Your Favorite Television Show?
    A. Any Answer Is Correct

13. Q. There is a five-letter word the pronunciation of which is not changed by removing four of the successive vowels. What is it?
    A. No Answer Is Correct

14. Q. What Is Your Favorite Cartoon Character?
    A. Any Answer Is Correct

15. Q. In a certain hamlet there is a single smooth-shaven barber who will only shave those people who do not shave themselves. Who shaves the barber?
    A. No Answer Is Correct

16. Q. What Is Your Favorite Day Of The Week?
    A. Any Answer Is Correct

17. Q. The square root of this number when added to the square root of the second number exactly doubles the first number. What is the second number?
    A. No Answer Is Correct

First Impressions! Lasting Impressions!

LASTING IMPRESSIONS! Closings You Can Count On

Crazy Quiz

18. Q. What is your favorite time of day?
    A. Any Answer Is Correct

19. Q. A man owns eight jumping dogs. Three of the dogs can jump four feet, four of the dogs can jump three feet, and one of the dogs can jump only one foot. How many of the dogs can jump higher than the average jumping height of all the dogs?
    A. No Answer Is Correct

20. Q. What is your name?
    A. Any Answer Is Correct

Certificate Of Outstanding Achievement

This Award Is Presented To

_____

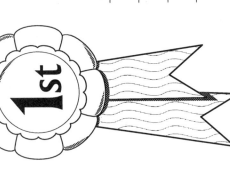

FOR ACHIEVING

FIRST PLACE

_____ _____
DATE   SIGNATURE

30   LASTING IMPRESSIONS! Closings You Can Count On

LASTING IMPRESSIONS! Closings You Can Count On

VIDEO CARD TRICK!

The trainer finishes the session with a card trick performed by a great magician from the past.

The magician's voice on the tape (either audio or video) gives instructions as a volunteer follows those instructions with a deck of cards.

Unbelievable as it seems, the card selected by the volunteer is revealed to him by the voice on the tape!

In fact, the card selected by the volunteer is the very message card needed to summarize the material under discussion!

In preparing for this magic trick, select a card from your Magic Memory Deck whose question will summarize your training content.

If you can't find exactly what you want, go ahead and make a suitable card from a matching deck.

Place the card face down on top of the face down Magic Memory Deck.

Now choose a word or short phrase that will also help capsulize the main emphasis of your training session. A word or phrase with about ten letters is perfect (i.e. Customer First, Cost Control, Sale And Service, etc.). Hold the deck face down in your hand (your content summary card is still on top) and spell your word or phrase one letter at a time—laying one card on the table from the top of the deck for each letter you're spelling.

Then spell the word again from the deck—continuing to place more cards on the first tabled pile from the deck.

Pick up this tabled pile of cards without disturbing their order and drop the pile face down on top of the deck you still hold in your hand.

You have now placed the important content summary card in the deck at a specific position from the top. Your content card is twice as many cards down from the top of the deck as you have in your content word or phrase.

First Impressions! Lasting Impressions!

32 LASTING IMPRESSIONS! Closings You Can Count On

Video Card Trick!

In other words, if you have five letters in your content word or phrase, your content card is now ten cards down from the top of the deck.

You are now ready to begin your presentation!

You might want to consider introducing this as a trick you got inside a cereal box when you were a kid. Inside the box was a small record with an unbelievable card trick. Your mom saved the record and you've transferred it to cassette tape so that you could share it now with your training group. If you're young enough, it could even be a video cassette!

Have a person come to the front of the room as you turn on the cassette. The script for the tape should be something like this:

> "Hello boys and girls! This is Mr. Magic ready to share with you a magic trick from the repertoire of the professionals! The name of this trick is 'The Famous Card Trick!' I think you're going to like it!
>
> The first thing you need to get is a deck of cards. Do you have a deck of cards?
> Gooooooooooooooooooooood!
>
> Hold the deck of cards face down in either your right or left hand.
>
> (Watch to make sure your volunteer is doing it correctly. If there's a problem, go over and help him follow the directions.)
>
> We are now going to mix the cards in a special way! Reach up with the hand not holding the deck and remove a few cards from the top of the deck. Don't take more than eight or nine cards and don't tell me how many you took! Shuffle the cards you've just taken. (Pause) Now hide those cards! (Pause) Have you done all that?
> Goooooooooooooooooooooood!
>
> Next I want you to take cards from the top of the deck and spell an important word (phrase). Take one card from the deck for each letter in the word (phrase) and lay it face down on the table.

LASTING IMPRESSIONS! Closings You Can Count On

Video Card Trick!

"The word I want you to spell is _____ (your chosen training word).

Let's do the spelling letter by letter...

_____ _____ _____ _____
_____ _____

(Here you will actually spell the word—giving the volunteer enough time to lay a card on the table for each letter you give.)

Remember those cards you took from the deck and shuffled at the beginning? Well, bring them out now and add them to the top of the deck. (Pause) Have you done that?
Gooooooooooooooooooooood!

Now let's do the spelling again. Lay down more cards on the table for each letter.

(Again on the tape you spell the word letter by letter—giving the volunteer enough time to lay a card on the table for each letter you give.)

Place the deck aside now and pick up the last card you dealt to the table. Concentrate on the number and suit of the card you've selected and I will attempt to read your mind.

If my magic is working well today...I believe you chose (dramatic pause) the _____ of _____ (the number and suit of your special content card).

However, even more important than the card you picked is what's written on the back of the card...since _____ (the content information you desired) really does summarize the main point of this training session! Thank you for your help!"

ADDITIONAL IDEAS might include using a musical background on the cassette tape (Circus music sounds great!) to give it that authentic childhood feel!

First Impressions! Lasting Impressions!

34 LASTING IMPRESSIONS! Closings You Can Count On

LASTING IMPRESSIONS! Closings You Can Count On

FINGERTIP VANISH!

The trainer holds the deck of review cards in his hand and asks any person to name any card in the deck, and it will be made to vanish!

The trainer squeezes the deck in his hand and indeed the ENTIRE DECK disappears without a trace...right at his fingertips!

This shocking trick can be used very well to conclude a training session. As the trainer vanishes the deck, he makes a tossing motion towards the trainees indicating that the information in the deck has now been transferred into the minds of the learners. The deck is no longer needed.

It's a very powerful way to get rid of the review deck at the end of the session!

After you've used the Magic Memory Deck for a review as described previously in this book, you simply hold the deck at your fingertips, and it disappears!

In order to present this most memorable ending to your training session, you'll need to take about ten minutes to make a special gimmick.

Using an unlined index card, cut a piece from the index card that measures ⅝" x the same width as a single card from your Magic Review Deck. Poker size cards are approximately 2½" wide and bridge size cards are about 2¼" wide.

You are now going to make this little piece of index card look like the end of a complete deck of cards. It's easy to do.

Take a good pen (an Ultra Fine Flair works great) and a ruler. Draw a series of lines lengthwise across the piece of index card.

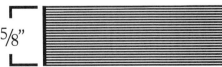

After the ink has dried, carefully run an eraser over the ink several times to take some of the boldness out of the lines. The lines must be muted and soft.

LASTING IMPRESSIONS! Closings You Can Count On

Fingertip Vanish!

Using transparent tape, hinge this piece of index card to the very end of the Joker from your Magic Memory Deck. Put the transparent tape hinge on the *FACE* of the card and the *BACK* of the index card piece.

Now fold the index piece down at right angles to the end of the card and with a cursory glance, it should pass as the end of the deck.

To further heighten the illusion, taper the two ends of the fake piece. Start at the card and slightly cut both ends tapering them from top to bottom.

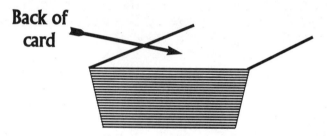

When you get ready to conclude the training session, use both hands to reach into your open briefcase and bring this special card out in one hand face down with the face of the card parallel to your upturned palm. Your thumb and index finger should be holding either end of the fake piece.

FIGURE #8   The other fingers of your hand should curl naturally around the side of the card with the tips of the fingers resting on the back of the card. The bottom of the fake piece should rest against your hand (see FIGURE #8).

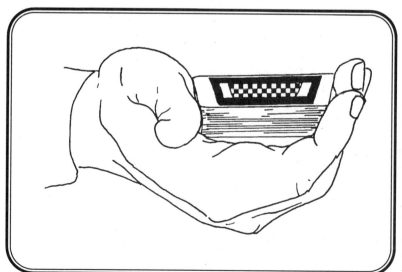

Remember that the group has seen you use this deck of cards throughout the

LASTING IMPRESSIONS! Closings You Can Count On

Fingertip Vanish!

training! If you don't draw undue attention to the deck, they will assume it to be the same deck you've been using! Take time to look in a mirror and build your confidence in how great the illusion really looks!

As a final act of review, ask anyone in the group to name any card in the deck. You claim that you will make it disappear!

After someone has called out a card, tell the group that first you must remove the joker. Reach around the front of the deck with your free hand—slipping your fingers under the fake with your thumb resting on top of the card.

You will now do two things simultaneously. Use the fingers of your free hand to fold the fake piece under the card—removing that card WHILE you turn over the hand originally holding the card. You may also need to turn your body at this time so that the back of the hand that once held the "deck" is now facing the audience. The hand should remain cupped as though it still contained the deck (FIGURE #9).

The action in this last paragraph should appear as though you simply reached over and removed one card from the deck and now you hold the deck in your hand with the back of that facing the audience.

Briefly show the face of the Joker. Your fingers should adequately cover the fake piece. Put the Joker away in your pocket. Turn all attention to your still cupped other hand.

FIGURE #9

Suddenly, get an inspiration! Tell the class that since they've done such a good job of learning the material, you really don't need ANY of the cards anymore!

LASTING IMPRESSIONS! Closings You Can Count On

Fingertip Vanish!

Squeeze your hand into a fist and make a tossing motion towards your class! The entire deck will appear to have vanished!

Thank the class for their attention and take your much deserved bows for being such a creative trainer!

A special thank you to Paul Harris, creator of this routine, for his permission to include it in this book.

BIOGRAPHY OF THE AUTHOR

DAVE ARCH

Author of the books in the Tricks for Trainers Resource Library including *Tricks for Trainers, Volume I & II* as well as *First Impressions/Lasting Impressions*. Dave Arch has pioneered the use of magic in his motivational programs and training.

Since 1982, magic has proven itself an effective communication tool for groups as diverse as hospital CEO's to sales representatives to banking administrators.

Combining a ten year background in personal and family counseling with a professional expertise in magic, Dave travels from his home in Omaha, Nebraska, to present his unique presentations before some 25,000 people each year in both corporate and conference settings.

Whether he's using a power saw to saw an audience volunteer in half or attempting to escape from a regulation straitjacket, his audiences long remember both the excellent content and the entertaining audience involvement that have become the trademakrs of his successful presentations.

ROBERT W. PIKE, CSP

Robert has developed and implemented training programs for business, industry, government and the professions since 1969. As founder and CEO of Creative Training Techniques International, Inc., and Creative Training Techniques Press, Bob leads sessions over 150 days per year covering topics of leadership, attitudes, motivation, communication, decision-making, problem-solving, personal and organizational effectiveness, conflict management, team building and managerial productivity. More than 60,000 trainers have attended the Creative Training Techniques™ workshop. As a consultant, Bob has worked with such organizations as Pfizer, UpJohn, Caesar Boardwalk Regency, Exhibitor Magazine, Hallmark Cards and IBM.

Over the years Bob has contributed to magazines like "TRAINING," "The Personal Administrator," and "The Self-Development Journal." He is editor of the "Creative Training Techniques Newsletter" and is author of *"The Creative Training Techniques Handbook,"* and *"Improving Managerial Productivity."*

WIN *Rave Reviews* on your next **Presentation**

"I have never felt so enthusiastic about a program! This workshop is a MUST for any trainer, regardless of level of experience."

Susan Russell, Bank One

Do you talk so people really listen?

Bob Pike's Creative Training Techniques™ Seminar

Find out why over 65,000 trainers love Creative Training Techniques. What makes this seminar so different? You'll learn how to get your participants enthusiastically involved in the training. By creating an interactive learning environment, you'll watch the attendees excitement go up and up and up. The result? Your group will easily learn twice as much. When they apply their new skills on the job, you'll see dramatic results.

Learn a revolutionary training approach—Participant-Centered Training. This teaching style is far more effective than traditional lecture-based training. Over 65,000 trainers world-wide have attended this seminar and applied these participant-centered training techniques to their work environments. More effective training means a more valuable and effective work force. Register today so you can get rave reviews on your next presentation. Over 140 public seminars are scheduled in 40 different cities each year.

In-house Training Seminars

Customized programs for trainers, sales staff, and technical presenters developed for 100s of organizations. Give us a call so we can discuss how to help your company increase work force performance by maximizing the impact of your training. Just a few of our clients who have brought Creative Training Techniques programs in-house:

American Express • AT&T • GE Plastics • State Farm Insurance • 3M • Tonka Corporation

Creative Solutions Catalog
Insider's Tips to Double the Impact of Your Presentation

Filled with fun, stimulating, creative resources including games, magic, music, wuzzles, books, tapes, videos, software, presentation graphics—everything you need to make your presentation an absolute winner.

1-800-383-9210
www.cttbobpike.com

Creative Training Techniques International, Inc. • 7620 W. 78th Street, Mpls. MN 55439 • (612) 829-1954 • Fax (612) 829-0260

Bob Pike's
Creative Training Techniques™ Train-the-Trainer Conference

The only conference dedicated exclusively to the participant-centered approach to training

- Learn about the revolutionary, participant-centered training approach—the breakthrough alternative to lecture-based training
- See the nation's leading training consultants model their very best participant-centered activities
- Experience the power of participant-centered techniques to dramatically increase retention
- Learn about innovative training transfer techniques adopted by leading Fortune 500 companies
- Discover powerful management strategies that clearly demonstrate the business results for your training programs

Just a few of the companies who have sent groups (not just individuals) to the Conference

American Express • AT&T • Caterpillar • First Bank
Southern Nuclear Operating Company • State Farm • United HealthCare • US West

Rave Reviews!

"I refer to my conference workbook all the time. I've shared the techniques with my trainers, and my own evaluations have improved. Our needs analysis now produces actionable input. My comfort level with our line managers has increased—at my first meeting with them where I used what I learned at the conference, they applauded. Now that's positive feedback!"
  Gretchen Gospodarek, Training Manager, **TCF Bank Wisconsin**

"For any trainer who wants to move beyond lecture-based training, I recommend Bob Pike's participant-centered seminars and in-house consultants."
  Ken Blanchard, Co-Author of *The One-Minute Manager*

"Bob Pike is creating a new standard in the industry by which all other programs will soon be measured."
  Elliott Masie, President, **The MASIE Center**

Visit our Web site: www.cttbobpike.com to learn more about the Conference, Creative Training Techniques International, Inc. or the Participant-Centered Training approach.

1–800–383–9210
www.cttbobpike.com

Creative Training Techniques International, Inc. • 7620 W. 78th St., Mpls., MN 55439 • 612-829-1954 • Fax 612-829-0260

More great resources from Jossey-Bass/Pfeiffer!

End your sessions with a BANG!

Lynn Solem & Bob Pike

50 Creative Training Closers

They'll forget you as soon as you walk out the door—unless you make your training memorable. This essential resource is your way to make your mark. Fifty ways to close your training sessions and presentations so they won't forget you—or your training.

Many trainers start training sessions memorably with a rousing icebreaker, or with a spirited overview of what's to follow. But you're probably letting the ends slip through your fingers. Some trainers conclude training sessions by looking at their watches and saying, "Oh, time's up! Goodbye!" By trailing off with a whisper, you're missing an opportunity to reinforce your training. You're helping your participants to forget everything you've taught them. Stop this brain drain by ending with a bang! This invaluable book is packed with practical closers.

You get activities great for:

- *Reviewing* material
- *Celebrating* success
- *Motivating* participants . . . and more!

Solem and Pike show you all the essentials, and preparation is quick and easy. So little time to invest for such a HUGE payoff! This book is training dynamite—make it your secret weapon today.

paperback / 96 pages

50 Creative Training Closers
Item #F439

Bob Pike & Dave Arch

Dealing with Difficult Participants

127 Practical Strategies for Minimizing Resistance and Maximizing Results in Your Presentations

Everyone knows them . . . but almost no one knows how to deal with them. Difficult participants. The "latecomer." The "know-it-all." The "confused." What do you do? Train-the-trainer master Bob Pike and magician/trainer Dave Arch have the answers.

Learn to deal with types such as:

- The Preoccupied
- The Socializer
- The Introvert
- The Bored
- The Domineering
- The Unqualified
- The Skeptic
- The Sleeper . . . and others!

Don't let difficult participants get the best of you. You can't afford not to pick up this engaging book. Maximize the learning potential in all your presentations with *Dealing With Difficult Participants*!

paperback / 150 pages

Dealing with Difficult Participants
Item #F244

To order, please contact your local bookstore, call us toll-free at 1-800-274-4434, or visit us on the Web at www.pfeiffer.com.